THE NATIVE BRITISH SPOTTED PONY

CONTENTS

INTRODUCTION	2
HISTORY OF THE BREED IN BRITAIN	3
DEVELOPMENT AND DISTRIBUTION	6
OFFICIAL BREED PROFILE	9
GENERAL CHARACTER	9
TEMPERAMENT	9
CONSTITUTION	9
BREED CHARACTERISTICS	9
COLOUR	10
HEAD	11
NECK	11
SHOULDERS	12
FORELEGS	12
BODY	12
HINDQUARTERS	12
HIND LEGS	12
ACTION	12
THE VARIOUS COAT COLOURS EXPLAINED	12
OTHER BREED CHARACTERISTICS	16
TEMPERAMENT AND HEALTH	18
KEEPING AND FEEDING	20
PERFORMANCE AND THE NATIVE BRITISH SPOTTED PONY	21
TIPS ON BUYING	23
CONCLUSION	23

INTRODUCTION

Various types of spotted horses and ponies have existed throughout the world since time immemorial, and even today this wide geographic distribution is evidenced in many breeds including the Danish Knabstrup, the Appaloosa, the Pony of the Americas, the Colorado Ranger, the Australian Palouse Pony, the Mongolian Pony, the Libyan Leopard, some Falabellas, the Pinzgau strain of the Noriker in Austria and Bavaria, as well as the South German Coldblood. The same spotted coat pattern still exists at low frequency in the Welsh Pony, the Spanish Mustang and a host of Asian breeds such as the Karabair and the ponies from Tannu Tuva. It is important to make the distinction between recognised spotted breeds such as the Native British Spotted Pony, the Appaloosa, the Pony of the Americas and the Knabstrup, and other breeds where the spotted coat pattern is purely incidental to the breed and appears at random. Through history, equines with this

particular and unusual coat pattern have always been regarded as somewhat magical and mystical and, as such, the rightful steeds of royalty and noblemen. Several societies now exist both abroad and in this country which offer registration facilities for them. Of all the various spotted breeds, the true Native British Spotted Pony is arguably the most ancient, and its roots in Britain go back to well before the Bronze Age.

HISTORY OF THE BREED IN BRITAIN

The spotted pony was once a familiar sight on the heaths and in the forests of ancient Britain from the Ice Age onwards. At this time, England and France were one land mass, and cave paintings dating from 18,000 BC (*right*) at Peche-Merle in southwest France depict early man's impressions of the animals he hunted and which obviously had some mystical/religious influence on his life.

Similarly at Lascaux (Dordogne, France), Ice Age cave paintings (*below*) depicting bay, chestnut, piebald and spotted ponies ably demonstrate the incidence of spotted coat patterns across southern Europe at this time. You can estimate that these early spotted ponies would not have been more than about 12 hh by comparing them with the size of the cattle (aurochs, which often stood as high as five feet [15 hh]) and reindeer, which also appear in the same cave paintings.

The land mass forming Britain and France is believed to have been severed some time between 16,000 and 5,000 BC, after which time the British stock developed in isolation from the rest of Europe. The ponies thus enjoyed an entirely separate existence for at least 5,000 and possibly as much as 16,000 years. During this time our spotted ponies retained and consolidated a Celtic/Welsh appearance of a small pony with a neat head and dished face. You could be forgiven for thinking that the highly contrasting spotted

coat pattern made these ponies easy prey for predators. In reality, the spotted coat formed a natural protective camouflage in our ancient woods and heathlands.

The medieval period came before the development of a system of nomenclature based on breeds, so written records refer to the uses of equines rather than their breed names. The survival of the spotted pony during this period of history is amply demonstrated in paintings, tapestries, wall hangings and inventories. The Workshop Bestiary of 1187 AD shows a charming strong spotted rouncy from which our later Welsh pit ponies (now Welsh Section A) developed. Again, another spotted equus is depicted on the eleventh-century map of the world, the famous Mappa Mundi (*below*) in Hereford Cathedral. As you can see, British equi were longer legged than the British rounciès, and rather more the equivalent of today's riding pony or Welsh Section B.

The fact that British spotted ponies were always held in high esteem is illustrated in many ways. The written records of all the horses purchased for Edward I's campaign at Falkirk, dated 1298, included a spotted Welsh cob (then called a Powys), and not surprisingly this cob is one of the most expensive on the list.

In the fifteenth century, the manuscript 'Chronicles of Sir John Froissart' contains a picture titled 'The Duke of Gloucester Arrested by the Marshal and sent to Calais' (*opposite, top*). In this charming miniature

King Richard II rides away apparently unconcerned, and the coloured original shows the courtier to his right is riding a beautiful little spotted chestnut cob.

Also from the fifteenth century, this detail (*right*) taken from a miniature painted in 1490 in Writhe's Garter Book shows a new Knight of the Bath on a spotted mount riding through the courtyard of the Tower of London to present himself to the King.

Perhaps most significantly, the power of the horse has historically been acknowledged through the Celtic worship of the goddess Epona, and continued to this day through our morris dancing and mummers plays, in which the spotted hobbyhorse represents spring growth and fertility.

DEVELOPMENT AND DISTRIBUTION

In medieval times, harsh laws were passed against the smaller ponies at a time when the Crown pronounced that 'our knights should be better mounted'. This coincided with the change from chain mail to full armour, when our traditional rouncies were no longer able to carry the increased weight. Although many of our smaller ponies were rounded up for slaughter in favour of the imported destriers or warhorses, many of the spotted ponies were warmly welcomed by the gypsy fraternity to supplement their colourful piebald and skewbald ponies. However, both very distinct colours can also become mixed in the 'pintaloosa' (a colour which surprisingly is much prized in America) which carries both genes and is thus only partly spotted.

Despite all the laws and prejudices, the spotted coat pattern continued to be accepted by the Welsh right up to at least 1925, when a spotted colt won the Breed Championship at the Royal Welsh Show of that year. In spite of later bans, the spotted coat pattern still infrequently appears in a few pure-bred Welsh blood-lines even to the present day, as illustrated by this pure-bred Welsh spotted mare (*top right*). This blanket-spotted colt pony (*bottom right*) being shown in-hand at the Three Counties Show is of Welsh-type. However, as most of the emerging modern British breed societies, which were established around the first quarter of the twentieth century, decided no longer to accept our traditional spotted ponies as one of their acceptable standard colours, the net effect was that the numbers of our important British breed started to fall to an all-time record low.

In order to try to redress the balance, just after the Second World War in 1947, the first British Spotted Horse and Pony Society was formed by enthusiasts seeking to continue and re-establish our spotted heritage and, towards this end, those first enthusiasts acquired their start-up stock from the gypsies

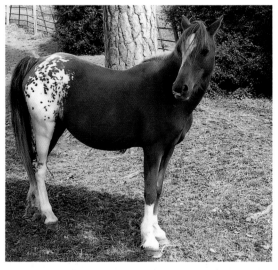

and from local markets. Later, the breeders of the spotted horses took a decision to form a breed society of their own and set up the British Appaloosa Society to represent their interests, the ponies (*top*, British Spotted Ponies) continuing under the name of the British Spotted Pony Society. More recently still, those members who wished to continue to keep the breed as a truly native breed, as determined by bloodline rather than country of birth, formed the Spotted Pony Breed Society (GB).

Many of the original gypsy-type ponies gathered together by the early enthusiasts lacked good conformation and, in order to redress this deficiency and put the spots back where they have always rightfully belonged, the Society deliberately encouraged out-crossing to virtually all ponies registered with established native British breed societies. This far-sighted policy quickly started to provide new generations of well-spotted ponies of much better conformation than hitherto, in all sizes from miniatures (such as this miniature spotted stallion [*middle*] of good conformation) up to 14.2 hh; this British Spotted Pony filly (*bottom*) is 13 hh.

More recently still, after breeding for good conformation had become the prime objective above breeding for the spotted coat colour, it was decided, in the interests of breeding to type, to limit the former very liberal out-crossing policy to just four breeds, namely Shetlands, Dartmoors, Welsh (all sections up to 14.2 hh) and British Riding Ponies registered with the National Pony Society. Out-crossing to fully registered ponies of these breeds is still encouraged at the present time as numbers of our own progeny do not yet justify us becoming a 'closed breed'. This colt foal of good conformation (*above*) is the result of mating a British Spotted Pony stallion to a British Riding Pony mare. This enlightened

policy has already seen the most dramatic improvement in quality, conformation and what geneticists call hybrid vigour over the last two decades and, as a direct result, our ponies can now rival other breeds at both national and international level.

AUTHOR'S TIP

As our ponies range from miniatures (*below right*) up to 14.2 hh (this British Spotted Pony filly [*below left*] will make 13 hh) our breed profile is, of necessity, very general and designed primarily to describe a pony of good conformation. Conformation always comes first and spots last on our list of priorities and, indeed, our judges are now required in the first instance to judge our ponies 'as if they were all black', only taking the coat pattern into consideration if two ponies are otherwise thought to be of equal merit.

In terms of distribution, our membership is spread and our breed is now recognised not only throughout Britain but also abroad, where our hardy native ponies are much prized. Our registered British Spotted Ponies are the envy of much of the rest of the world, and exports have taken place to most countries, especially to America, Australia, Switzerland and the rest of Europe.

OFFICIAL BREED PROFILE

GENERAL CHARACTER

A quality pony with adequate bone and substance, hardy and active with real pony character of small, riding or cob type, up to and including 14.2 hh.

TEMPERAMENT

Native British Spotted Ponies are renowned for having a courageous yet kind, loving and tractable nature.

(This kind amenable four-year-old mare [*right*] is handled by her nine-year-old owner.)

CONSTITUTION

The Society places great importance on native hardiness and the ability to live out, even in the severest of British winters.

BREED CHARACTERISTICS

All ponies *must* display at least one or more of the following:

White sclera round the eye.

Mottled skin This part-dark, part-pink skin is usually most evident around the genitals, lips, muzzle, eyes and inside the ear.

Striped hooves.

COLOUR

Leopard Spots of any colour on a white or light-coloured background. (This is a well-marked black spotted leopard stallion.)

Fewspot White base coat with only a few spots or, in rare cases, with a complete absence of spots. Strong spotted characteristics are often accompanied by varnish marks (groupings of dark hairs within an area, usually the nose, cheekbones, stifle, gaskin and knee). (A fewspot stallion.)

Snowflake White spots on a dark base coat. (A British Spotted Pony snowflake gelding.)

OFFICIAL BREED PROFILE • 11

Blanket An area of white over the hips and hindquarters, with or without spots, on any base colour. The blanket can extend over the entire back and shoulders.

Mottled pattern The coat is most often irregularly ticked with white, also having large or small roan spots, with rather blurred outlines. Sometimes a coat looks like an ordinary roan coat in which dark blots appear. (*Below,* a roan-based British Spotted Pony colt.)

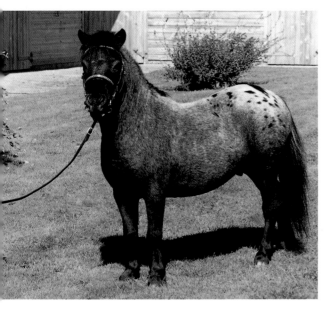

Solid colours are eligible for a separate register but must be of proven spotted breeding, and preferably show some breed characteristics.

Piebald and skewbald markings of any kind are not eligible, nor are the progeny of piebald and skewbald ponies accepted for registration.

HEAD

Full of quality and true pony character. Big bold and alert eyes set well apart. Ears should be well placed, small, neat and in proportion to the head. Prominent, open nostrils. Clean, well-defined throat. A coarse head and roman nose are to be discouraged. Teeth and jaw should be correct.

NECK

Should have good length and be well carried. Moderately lean in mares, but inclined to be more cresty in stallions.

SHOULDERS

Good, strong, sloping and well laid back. Withers should be well defined but not 'knifey'.

FORELEGS

Should be set square and true. Not tied-in at the elbow. Long strong forearms with well-developed knees. Short flat bone below the knee. Pasterns of proportionate length and slope. Well-shaped dense hoofs.

BODY

Muscular, strong, well coupled with plenty of heart room. Good deep girth and well-sprung ribs.

HINDQUARTERS

Lengthy, strong, well muscled, not ragged or drooping, with well set-on tail.

HIND LEGS

Well let-down hocks, large flat clean bone, prominent points. The hock not to be

set behind a line from the point of quarter to fetlock joint. No sickle or cow hocks. Pasterns to be of proportionate length and slope. Hoofs well shaped and dense.

ACTION

Low, straight from the shoulder, free flowing. Hocks well flexed with straight action coming well under the body. (This British Spotted Pony [*below*] demonstrates its free-flowing action at the Three Counties Show.)

THE VARIOUS COAT COLOURS EXPLAINED

Each of a horse's characteristics is controlled by thousands of pairs of genes situated along pairs of chromosomes (one of which the horse inherits from each of its parents), and geneticists will tell you that the spotted coat pattern is caused by 'one autosomal [i.e. non-sex linked] dominant gene'. If the pony inherits just one gene responsible for spotting from either of its parents then it will be spotted.

In fact, the spotted gene should really be looked upon as a whitening gene because its action is to leach out the predetermined base colour of bay, black or chestnut, leaving islands of that same original colour, often intensified. Occasionally the residual spots of colour thus produced will also be rimmed by halos, ghosts or shadows around the spots themselves, and this most attractive and unusual effect is caused either by a band of roaning round the spot or an extended area of the underlying skin being sufficiently dark to show through the white hair above.

If the pony has a pair of genes both coded 'spotted', this double dose of the whitening effect means that it will carry hardly any spots at all and will be nearly cream or white all over with white feet. This is known to us as a genetic fewspot and is one of the most genetically valuable ponies Society members possess because, if you mate a true genetic fewspot with any solid coloured pony you are guaranteed to get a spotted foal every single time. One of my many stallions is such a genetic fewspot and he has now produced well over 150 fully spotted progeny when mated only with solid-coloured females. The leopard spotted filly foal (*above*) with her solid-coloured dam is by a fewspot stallion.

The only apparent drawback is that these fewspot ponies have an unusually large amount of pink skin around the nostrils and eyes, as illustrated by this headshot of a fewspot mare. This means that owners have to watch out for sunburn in the summer months (*see* page 20) and rainscald in winter. The lack of pigmentation can also affect their eyesight to some degree, but any such defect is not thought to be passed on to their fully spotted progeny after some colour has been returned.

This peculiarity of the genes on the chromosomal pair being different in order to produce the most 'characteristic' leopard-spotted coat colour makes the British Spotted Pony what is known as a heterozygous breed, and as such it can never breed true as compared with some other spotted animals, such as Dalmatian dogs. Two Dalmations

mated together will always produce spotted Dalmation progeny, whereas the result of mating two spotted ponies together will be far more unpredictable, as outlined in the following paragraph. There are in fact many such heterozygous breeds, including Dexter cattle and, for coat colour in particular, both the Dairy Shorthorn and Blue Albion breeds of cattle.

Spotted ponies can thus be all colours, white, spotted and solid-coloured, the two latter in the three main colours of bay, black and chestnut. Even if one breeds a leopard-spotted pony with another leopard-spotted pony it can never be guaranteed that you will end up with spotted progeny as, on average, a quarter will be solid coloured. In exactly the same way as a genetic fewspot is basically white because it has received a double dose of the spotted gene, it is equally possible for the resultant foal to receive a similar double dose of the equivalent gene coded 'non-spotted', in which case that foal will remain solid-coloured throughout its life and be unable to pass on any spots to future generations. In terms of genetic probability, if you mate a spotted pony with a solid-coloured pony you will have a 50 per cent chance of the offspring being spotted, but in a spotted to spotted mating that chance will be increased to 75 per cent.

All horse owners will know the three basic colours of bay, black and chestnut. The three photos show spotted versions of all three colours: a bay spotted foal (top), a black spotted foal (middle), and a chestnut spotted gelding (bottom). They are all by one of my stallions who is one of the very rare examples of a loudly marked harlequin leopard spot, and from the photo at the top of page 15 you will be able to see that in addition to the three basic colours he has roan spots and halos, and does, therefore,

display the full range of markings! The mechanism underlying this unusual but attractive phenomenon is still being researched.

Please note that the photo of the black spotted foal was taken on the day of his birth and he was therefore actually born a full leopard spot. However, just to complicate matters, the spotted gene also seems to carry a built-in time clock, rather like the human hair greying gene, and whilst a few foals will be born as full leopards, the vast majority only develop this pattern over the years. The foal may be born completely solid coloured, or with only a few white hairs, but beneath the solid-coloured coat a full spotted pattern may be revealed as early as the change-of-foal-coat stage (*middle*). Again, some may be born either as a snowflake or else 'snowflake-out' over the next few months of their life. Often when snowflaking occurs the white 'snowflakes' gradually become larger until they coalesce and then the underlying solid-colour spots gradually start to show as islands of colour. This filly (*bottom*) shows progressive snowflaking. If the time clock is even more advanced, the pony may be born with a spotted blanket but, in most cases, this will extend forwards over the early years of life until the pony becomes a near leopard or a full leopard.

From this simple explanation you will understand that most of our ponies carrying one gene coded 'spotted' become leopards over time, and that the other patterns should generally be regarded as transitional only. The exact mechanism is not as yet fully understood but, again, just like the timing of the onset of grey hair in humans, tends to run in families. This loudly marked leopard-spotted stallion (*right*) was born apparently solid black and did not even start showing signs of any spotting until he was four or five years old. You can imagine that the breeder was only too keen to buy him back when he found out!

OTHER BREED CHARACTERISTICS

The spotted gene does not create traditional coat spotting in isolation but is also responsible for a number of physical characteristics which, more often than not, accompany the spotted coat. These are white sclera, striped hooves, parti-coloured skin and varnish marks.

White sclera round the eye, often known as 'humanoid eye', makes the eye of a spotted pony resemble the human eye. A horse or pony that shows the white of its eye is often dubbed a menacing equine but in the case of the spotted pony this white sclera is indicative of its spotted pedigree and not its personality, which is normally both placid and tractable.

Striped hoofs range from mainly blue feet with a thin white stripe, to wide, evenly spaced white and black stripes, through to the wholly white feet of fewspot ponies with

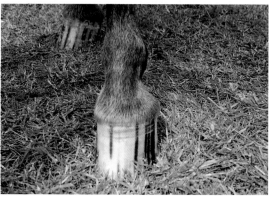

the double dose of the spotting gene. Here these stripes can be seen developing on a foal's foot.

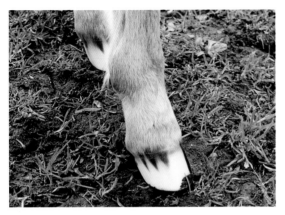

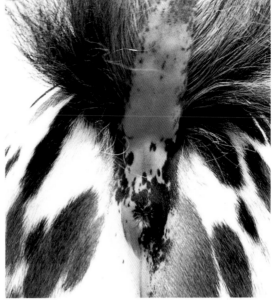

Parti-coloured skin refers to the mottled pink and black colouration on the skin, most clearly visible around the mouth (as exhibited by this snowflake stallion [*below*]), the genitalia and under the dock (shown clearly on this gelding [*top right*]) but also present on the skin underneath the coat hair. In fact, close inspection with an ophthalmoscope reveals that even the back of the eyeball is mottled!

All these secondary breed characteristics may again develop as the pony matures and the spotted time clock is activated. All these characteristics may also be present in some of our 'solid coloured' spotted ponies.

Varnish marks (*below*) are a collection of dark hairs, which highlight the elbows, knees and stifle. Spotted ponies often display varnish marks. Like the Appaloosa breed of horse some of our ponies also have a sparse mane and tail, for which at present there is no show ring penalty.

TEMPERAMENT AND HEALTH

The breed is well recognised as having a wonderfully tractable temperament, whilst at the same time being very courageous; British Spotted Ponies will attempt any task set by their owners. By way of illustration, my own spotted pony driving team was never known to refuse a hazard in its entire seven years of tough competition and are shown here keen to take the plunge at a water hazard. All this, coupled with a high amount of native cunning makes the

Society members' ponies ideal as children's mounts (*left*), for driving – the unicorn of British Spotted Ponies (*opposite, top left*) is being shown in front of Her Majesty the Queen at the British Driving Society's Show, Windsor – for showing, or merely as loving companions. If you love them and treat them with respect, they will repay you in full.

No one could be immune to the charms of the remaining three pictures opposite; a very pretty snowflake mare (*top right*), a spotted 'poorly patient' collecting for Cancer Relief MacMillan Nurses (*bottom left*), and a spotted pony 'all dressed up' for the show ring (*bottom right*).

Because they are so innately sensible, many owners let their mares foal quite naturally out in the field, and one 'deprived' owner recently reported that out of some thirty-odd foalings without incident he had never actually had the privilege of seeing one born!

As our ponies originated from our ancient Mountain and Moorland breeds, another innate characteristic, being able to thrive in the most adverse of conditions, means that veterinary visits (and bills!) are generally kept to the minimum consistent with good management.

KEEPING AND FEEDING

The constitution of our spotted ponies is so tough (the smaller ones in particular having coats up to four inches thick) that they can be outwintered in almost the harshest of our English winters, and many of our members have many more ponies than available stables. Rugging-up is seldom required, although this may be considered a sensible precaution for those ponies, particularly of the show-pony type, who contain a higher percentage of hot blood in their pedigree. This pony (*top right*) lives out at the highest point of Rutland.

Spotted ponies thrive on a high-fibre diet of grass in summer and good hay in winter. Brood-mares, foals and ponies who are consistently worked, may need supplementary feeding, but even this should resemble the high-fibre low-protein make-up of the natural native pony diet.

Apart from regular worming, trimming of hooves and teeth rasping, the only real precaution owners of spotted ponies must take is to see that some natural or artificial shelter is available in hot sunny weather when sunburn can affect the pink skin around the nose and eyes. This photosensitivity is heightened if there is an excess of buttercups in the pasture (*bottom right*).

The top picture on page 21 shows a spotted pony being hot-shod by the blacksmith at the Three Counties Show. You will

note that his thirteen-year-old handler looks very nonchalant even when the hot shoe itself is applied, but this particular pony has been through it all time and time again as he is now some twenty-eight years old. This veteran has attended all our Breed Shows since they first started in 1984 and has been a consistent winner.

Spotted ponies are no different from other equines in that they need constant access to a clean supply of water and have a liking for mineral licks, which make up for the imbalances in the forage minerals. Every responsible owner must also have ready access to stabling in case of illness or emergency.

PERFORMANCE AND THE NATIVE BRITISH SPOTTED PONY

The breed excels in all disciplines and the following photographs show our members jumping, driving, riding and enjoying their ponies.

Karen Bassett drove our spotted pony team to success between 1983 and the team's retirement in 1991. During this time the team was voted Team of the Year at the Horse of the Year Show, won the Benelux Trophy for the best team in Europe, as well as taking the National Championships for four of those years. In all, Karen won no less than six International Grand Prix all over Europe, and thus was able to enhance the standing of our native spotted ponies worldwide.

These British Spotted Ponies are enjoying other activities: the Bassett family's Broomells Ming achieving a clear round (*top right*); a pair scurrying at high speed at the Royal Show (*top left*); a small spotted pony with his spotted 'equine' companions in a charioteer race (*middle right*); one of the larger British Spotted mares, Tequila Sunrise, ridden out on a pleasure hack by her owner Gaye Dalley (*middle left*), and (*bottom right*) the rare sight of a British Spotted Pony random at the British Driving Society Annual Show, Windsor.

TIPS ON BUYING

Not every magazine or newspaper has spotted ponies for sale. The easiest way to purchase a British Spotted Pony is through the Society's sales list which contains all the members' ponies for sale.

The most obvious pitfall to avoid when buying a spotted pony is that of purchasing a 'fader', i.e. a pony that has grey in its colour genes. In this case, when the initial coat colour starts to fade, the pony will lose all the cherished and often striking spots and eventually turn pure white! Fortunately this phenomena is now understood by our members and, as a result, they tend to avoid breeding from all grey ponies. Nevertheless it is a wise precaution to ask to see the pony's parents if possible and, if not, be provided with photographs of them.

Buyers primarily interested in breeding, riding, driving or showing are much more likely to obtain the results they want from a pony of well-known and authenticated pedigree, such as Katie Tinklin's Haw Lhotse (*right*), as inherited predictability is the whole purpose of our stud book.

The Spotted Pony Breed Society of Great Britain is the only society to embrace the concept of a truly British native breed of spotted pony and, as a consequence, ponies registered in our studbooks are sought after throughout the rest of the world, not only for their wondrous coat patterns, but also for those virtues of true native hardiness, conformation, temperament and stamina which make our native ponies unique. To be eligible for our Main Register our ponies must prove a minimum of 87.5 per cent native British blood, although in practice the majority of our ponies on this register have well above this figure, and our standards are becoming more stringent the whole time.

CONCLUSION

The British Spotted Pony with its exotic coat pattern has been around for many thousands of years and, during that time, it has, like most truly British breeds, had some infusions of foreign blood, but the most important bloodlines come from the old Welsh hill ponies and cobs. It has also been miniaturised by some studs using the hardy Shetland Pony blood.

Throughout its ancient ancestry, the attractive and unusual markings of the spotted pony have made it the subject of myths and legends but its toughness has ensured that it has survived to grace our fields today.

ACKNOWLEDGEMENTS

The author is grateful to all those who have so generously sponsored the production of this book both financially and by the provision of photographs and other help, and who have thus made it all possible, including in particular:

The Spotted Pony Breed Society (GB)
Secretary
Ms. Carol Ivory, 11 Instow Place, Llanrumney,
Cardiff, South Glamorgan CF3 5TN
Tel: (02920) 632334 Email: carol.ivory@ntlworld.com

Thanks to the following individuals: Mrs Julie Allen, Mrs Rosemary Bannister, Mrs Celia Birch, Mr and Mrs D. R. Cooper, Mrs Jenny Crickmore-Porter, Miss Jane Cullingford, Mrs Gaye Dalley, Mr and Mrs Tony Dennis, Mrs P. Formby, Miss Carol Ivory, Mrs Valerie Jackson, Mr Chris Jennings, Mr A. Rollo, Mrs Margaret Ruffell, Mrs Elizabeth Seymour, Mrs Sheila South, Mr Brian Taylor, Mrs Debbie Tinklin and Dr Jennifer Verity.

Where I have supplied photographs taken by others I have tried to identify the holders of any copyright and obtained the necessary permissions. In all other cases the members who have submitted photographs have been obliged to do likewise. Where the owners do not hold the copyright, I therefore wish to thank the following for permission to use photographs: Hilary Cotter; *Horse and Pony Magazine*; Leslie Lane; Noble Photos; Pleasure Prints; Real Time Imaging. And, finally, thanks to Hereford Cathedral for permission to reproduce the spotted equus from the Mappa Mundi.

British Library Cataloguing-in-Publication Data.
A catalogue record for this book is available from the British Library

ISBN 0.85131.799.5

Published in Great Britain in 2002 by
J. A. Allen an imprint of Robert Hale Ltd.,
Clerkenwell House, 45–47 Clerkenwell Green,
London EC1R 0HT

Design and Typesetting by Paul Saunders
Series editor Jane Lake
Colour processing by Tenon & Polert Colour Processing Ltd., Hong Kong
Printed in Malta by Gutenberg Press Limited